Steve Jobs and Apple

Andrea C. Nakaya

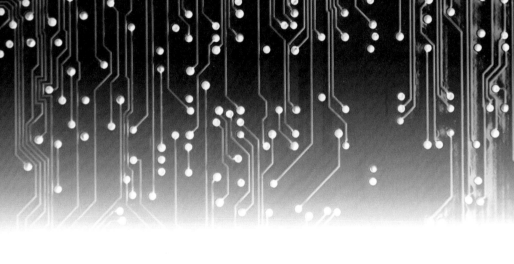

ReferencePoint Press®

San Diego, CA

© 2016 ReferencePoint Press, Inc.
Printed in the United States

For more information, contact:
ReferencePoint Press, Inc.
PO Box 27779
San Diego, CA 92198
www.ReferencePointPress.com

LIBRARY OF CONGRESS CATALOGING-IN-PUBLICATION DATA

Nakaya, Andrea C., 1976- author.
  Steve Jobs and Apple / by Andrea C. Nakaya.
    pages cm. -- (Technology titans)
  Includes bibliographical references and index.
  ISBN 978-1-60152-880-3 (hardback)
  ISBN 1-60152-880-9 (hardback)
  1. Jobs, Steve, 1955-2011--Juvenile literature. 2. Apple Computer, Inc.--History--Juvenile literature. 3. Computer engineers--United States--Biography--Juvenile literature. 4. Computer industry--History--Juvenile literature. I. Title.
  QA76.2.J63N35 2016
  621.39'092--dc23
  [B]

                                                            2014047677

Steve Jobs and the Digital Age

Today most people's lives are strongly tied to digital technology. Communication, entertainment, shopping, education, and a myriad of other activities frequently involve the use of computers and other digital devices. For example, smartphone owners use their phones to social network, check traffic or get directions, research restaurants or entertainment, transfer money or pay bills, check their calendars, listen to music, and many other things. Some people refer to this as a digital lifestyle. However, while most people take such reliance on digital technology for granted, it is actually a new phenomenon. Twenty-five years ago there was no such thing as Yelp for finding restaurant ratings or an app for checking the weather. The availability of this technology is due in part to a man called Steve Jobs. Jobs's innovative ideas and relentless drive to make them a reality have transformed society. As Bill Gates, former chief executive of Microsoft says, "The world rarely sees someone who has had the profound impact Steve has had, the effects of which will be felt for many generations to come."[1]

Predicting the Importance of Computers

In the 1970s Jobs had the unique ability to recognize how important computers and other digital technology would become to society, and he cofounded Apple Computer as a way of becoming part of that future. When he was younger, computers were large, intimidating machines that were far too expensive and complicated for the average person to use. However, he knew that this would change. Over time, computers shrank in size and became work, education, communication, and entertainment stations for more and more consumers. Back in 1985 he correctly predicted the major role that computers would play in people's lives in the future. In an interview given that year he argued,

> A computer is the most incredible tool we've ever seen. . . . There are no other tools that have the power and versatility of a computer. We have no idea how far it's going to go. Right now, computers make our lives easier. They do work for us in fractions of a second that would take us hours. They increase the quality of life, some of that by simply automating drudgery and some of that by broadening our possibilities. As things progress, they'll be doing more and more for us.[2]

Almost everyone who knew Jobs agrees that he was often an extremely difficult person to get along with. He demanded perfection and was very critical of others, and this angered many people. For example, in an early job at the Atari video game company, he caused so much conflict that he was given the night shift so that he would have minimal contact with his coworkers. *Rolling Stone* contributing editor Jeff Goodell first met Jobs in 1980 when he took a job at Apple. Goodell says, "Those who knew Jobs best and worked with him most closely—and I have talked to hundreds of them over the years—were always struck by his abrasive personality, his unapologetic brutality. He screamed, he cried, he stomped his feet. He had a cruelly casual way of driving employees to the breaking point and tossing them aside; few people ever wanted to work for him twice."[3] Walter Isaacson, author of the only authorized biography of Jobs, reports that even Jobs's wife, Laurene Powell, talked about his difficult personality. When Isaacson interviewed her, she told him, "There are parts of his life and personality that are extremely messy, and that's the truth." Powell stressed, "You shouldn't whitewash it."[4]

"The world rarely sees someone who has had the profound impact Steve has had, the effects of which will be felt for many generations to come."[1]

—Bill Gates, former chief executive of Microsoft Corporation.

A Man Who Changed the World

Yet despite the messy truth that Powell and many others talk about, most people speak about Jobs in an extremely positive way. This is because in addition to being critical and often frustrating to deal with, he was a brilliant and driven man who has had a huge impact on society. The devices and

According to many of those who knew him, Apple cofounder Steve Jobs was not an easy man to work with, but he was a brilliant innovator. His ideas left an indelible mark on technology and on daily life.

operating platforms that he helped create have changed technology forever. Apple iPhones, iPods, and Macintosh computers are in homes and businesses across the globe. When Jobs died in 2011 millions of people around the world mourned his loss. US president Barack Obama summed up the

feelings of many when he said, "Steve was among the greatest of American innovators brave enough to think differently, bold enough to believe he could change the world and talented enough to do it."[5]

Yet, while few people have equaled Jobs's accomplishments, his success did not come easily. Jobs worked very hard to achieve what he did. Throughout his life he faced many challenges and even some immense failures. However, Jobs never gave up trying to achieve what he believed in. He said, "My passion has always been to build an enduring company where people were motivated to make great products."[6] Throughout his life that is what he tried to do no matter how difficult it became. That perseverance, in addition to his extraordinary vision, made him a man who changed the world. Many people simply could not imagine their lives without the products that Jobs gave them.

Chapter 1

Early Life

Steve Paul Jobs was born on February 24, 1955, in San Francisco. His biological mother, Joanne Schieble, was from a Wisconsin family of German heritage. His biological father, Abdulfattah "John" Jandali, was a Muslim teaching assistant who came from Syria. Schieble and Jandali were both twenty-three years old, unmarried, and living in Wisconsin when they found out that Schieble was pregnant. They were not ready to have a child together, and Schieble's father disapproved of Jandali and threatened to disown her if she married him. Instead, Schieble travelled to San Francisco, where a doctor who took care of unwed mothers helped her arrange to have the baby adopted.

Adopted

Schieble's one requirement for adoption was that the parents be college graduates. Suitable college-graduate parents were found; however, at the last minute the pair changed their minds and decided they preferred to adopt a girl. Another set of prospective parents, Paul and Clara Jobs, offered to adopt Steve soon after. Neither had even graduated high school, and when Schieble found out, she initially refused to agree to the adoption. Schieble eventually relented only after the couple promised to pay for Steve's college education.

Some people say that because his birth parents gave him up for adoption, the sense of being abandoned was an important factor that shaped Jobs's life. For example, Chrisann Brennan, who mothered a child with Jobs, points out that he abandoned her and their daughter, Lisa. She insists that this was partly due to his being given up by his own parents, saying, "He who is abandoned is an abandoner."[7] However, Walter Isaacson, who interviewed Jobs numerous times, reports that Jobs did not feel this was true at all. Jobs told Isaacson that he actually grew up feeling that he was special. He said, "Knowing I was adopted may have made me feel more independent, but I have never felt abandoned. I've always felt special. My parents made me feel special."[8] According to Jobs, not only did his parents believe that he was special, but they went out of their way to accommodate his needs; for example, they moved to a different city so that he could go to a better school, and they sent him to one of the most expensive colleges in the country. However, Steve did not grow up alone in the Jobs household. Paul and Clara also adopted a daughter, Patty, when Steve was two years old.

> "He who is abandoned is an abandoner."[7]
>
> —Chrisann Brennan, mother of Lisa, Jobs's first daughter.

Lessons from His Father

Jobs's father, Paul, had a passion for mechanics and taught his son how to build things. Jobs said that his father could build anything they needed, such as a new cabinet or fence. He said, "My father, Paul, was a pretty remarkable man. . . . [He] worked very hard and was kind of a genius with his hands." According to Jobs, his father encouraged him to learn these skills:

> He had a workbench out in his garage where, when I was about five or six, he sectioned off a little piece of it and said "Steve, this is your workbench now." And he gave me some of his smaller tools and showed me how to use a hammer and saw and how to build things. It really was very good for me. He spent a lot of time with me . . . teaching me how to build things, how to take things apart, put things back together.[9]

In addition to teaching his son how to build things, Paul gave him an even more important lesson, which Jobs never forgot. Paul was a very careful craftsman, and even the small details were important to him. He taught his son the importance of doing things right, even if nobody else would know the difference. Jobs said, "He loved doing things right. He even cared about the look of the parts you couldn't see."[10] For example, his father taught him that even the back of a fence or cabinet should be made properly, despite the fact that nobody else could see it. Jobs applied that lesson to the products he later created. He insisted, "For you to sleep well at night, the aesthetic, the quality, has to be carried all the way through."[11]

Bored in School

Though Jobs was extremely smart, he did not fit well into the educational system. He just did not find his classes interesting, and he quickly became bored. Because Jobs was uninterested in his schoolwork, he frequently put his energy into things that got him in trouble. He particularly liked to play pranks. Jobs explained one famous prank. He said, "There was a big bike rack where everybody put their bikes, maybe a hundred bikes in this rack, and we traded everybody our lock combinations for theirs on an individual basis and then went out one day and put everybody's lock on everybody else's bike and it took them until about ten o'clock that night to get all the bikes sorted out."[12] In another prank, Jobs remembered making "Bring Your Pet to School Day" posters and causing chaos when students did actually bring their pets. He said, "It was crazy, with dogs chasing cats all over, and the teachers were beside themselves."[13] As a result of mischief such as this, he said, "we got kicked out of school a lot."[14] Despite such behavior, though, Jobs said he did not get in trouble with his parents. Instead, they blamed the teachers for not doing enough to engage Jobs. His father told the teachers, "If you can't keep him interested, it's your fault."[15]

> "For you to sleep well at night, the aesthetic, the quality, has to be carried all the way through."[11]
>
> —Steve Jobs.

In fourth grade, however, one teacher did manage to keep him interested. Imogene Hill approached Jobs with a deal; she gave him a math workbook and said that if he finished it and got 80 percent right, she would give him five dollars and some candy. Jobs said, "I looked at her like 'Are you crazy lady?' Nobody's ever done this before and of course I

The Jobs family moved to Los Altos, California, where Steve attended high school. The family's house (pictured) is on the city's list of historic places. Apple began in the family's garage.

did it." He said that soon he did not even need to be bribed in order to do the work she gave him. He remembered, "Before very long I had such a respect for her that it sort of re-ignited my desire to learn. . . . It was really quite wonderful. I think I probably learned more academically in that one year than I learned in my life."[16]

When the school finally had Steve tested and realized how smart he was, the administration recommended that he skip two grades, from the fourth into the seventh grade. His parents decided to have him skip only one grade. However, while skipping a grade made sense intellectually, Jobs found it socially difficult. Isaacson says, "The transition was wrenching. He was a socially awkward loner who found himself with kids a year older."[17] In addition, the middle school Jobs now found himself in was in a neighborhood with lots of gangs, and fights and bullying were common.

Steve Jobs's Biological Family

While Jobs said he always considered Paul and Clara Jobs to be his real parents, he was also interested in knowing more about his biological parents. As an adult, he managed to track them down. He discovered that not long after giving him up for adoption, Joanne Schieble and Abdulfattah Jandali got married and had a baby girl named Mona. Jandali then abandoned his wife and daughter a few years later. After finding out about his biological family, Jobs developed a relationship with both his mother and his sister Mona, but not with his father. According to biographer Walter Isaacson, Jobs had no interest in meeting Jandali. Jobs told Isaacson, "He didn't treat me well." In addition, he said, "What bothers me the most is that he didn't treat Mona well. He abandoned her." As an adult, Jobs did develop a strong relationship with Mona Simpson (Simpson was the name of Mona's stepfather). He said, "She's one of my best friends in the world. I call her and talk to her every couple of days." Like Jobs, Simpson also became successful in her chosen profession. Her first novel, *Anywhere but Here,* won the Whiting Prize and was adapted as a movie. She has also written a number of other books.

Quoted in Walter Isaacson, *Steve Jobs*, Simon & Schuster: New York, 2011, p. 256.
Quoted in Steve Lohr, "Creating Jobs," *New York Times*, January 12, 1997. www.nytimes.com.

In the middle of the year Jobs demanded that his parents put him in a different school. His parents gave in and managed to buy a house in nearby Los Altos, California, which was in a much better school district.

Friendship with Steve Wozniak

Jobs attended Cupertino Junior High, then Homestead High in Los Altos. While at Homestead High he met Steve Wozniak, or "Woz," who was a few years older than he, and the two developed a friendship that would change the future of computing. The two Steves became friends right away. Wozniak says that Jobs understood him in a way few others did.

"Typically, it was really hard for me to explain to people the kind of design stuff I worked on," he says, "But Steve got it right away. And I liked him. He was kind of skinny and wiry and full of energy."[18] Jobs also connected with Wozniak right away. "Woz was the first person I'd met who knew more about electronics than I did," he said. "I liked him right away."[19]

Later in their friendship, Jobs and Wozniak founded Apple Computer together. However, one of their earliest joint technological endeavors was something much simpler. Wozniak read an article detailing how hackers had learned to make long-distance phone calls for free with an electronic device called a blue box. This device replicated the tones that the phone service used to route long-distance calls. Wozniak and Jobs figured out how to make their own blue box, and after using the device for pranks— including calling the Vatican and trying to speak to the pope—they decided to make and sell the boxes for profit. The parts for the blue box cost about $40, and they sold the finished product for $150. According to Jobs, they made about one hundred blue boxes and sold most of them before they had second thoughts about this illegal business and decided to end it. However, Jobs said that the experience gave Wozniak and him the confidence that they could work together and create something important. He said, "It gave us a taste of what we could do with my engineering skills and his vision." In fact, Jobs insisted, "If it hadn't been for the Blue Boxes, there wouldn't have been an Apple."[20]

> "I liked [Steve Jobs]. He was kind of skinny and wiry and full of energy."[18]
>
> —Steve Wozniak, cofounder of Apple Computer with Jobs.

Growing Up in Silicon Valley

While Jobs was interested in technology from a young age, growing up in Silicon Valley also helped steer him into this field. Silicon is an element used to make a number of parts of electronic devices, and this part of the southern San Francisco Bay Area was named after this element because so many electronic technology companies are located there. Silicon Valley has a very high concentration of engineers and scientists, and it was the birthplace of many new inventions from companies such as Hewlett-Packard and Intel Corporation. Jeff Goodell talks about the powerful sense of possibility that helped fuel so many important inventions in Silicon Valley. He says that when Jobs was a boy, "The orchards that had covered the Valley had recently been bulldozed, and there was a sense of a new world rising, a belief that you could engineer your own future. There were no stuffy traditions, no cultural baggage. You could be whatever or whoever you wanted to be."[21]

While living in Los Altos, Jobs attended meetings for the Hewlett-Packard Explorers Club, and this also helped inspire him about the possibilities of technology. The Explorer's Club consisted of a small group of students that would meet in the cafeteria at Hewlett-Packard, where one of the company engineers would come and talk to them about what he was working on and show them the latest inventions. Jobs said that this is where he saw his first desktop computer. "It was called the 9100A, and it was a glorified calculator but also really the first desktop computer. It was huge, maybe forty pounds, but it was a beauty of a thing. I fell in love with it."[22]

College

In order to fulfill the promise that they would send him to college, Jobs's parents worked hard throughout his childhood to save for his college fund. There were many excellent and affordable colleges in California. For example, Wozniak went to nearby UC-Berkeley. However, when it came time for college, Jobs decided that he wanted to go to Reed College, a small liberal arts school in Portland, Oregon. Reed was known for attracting free-spirited youth, hippies, and those seeking to understand the meaning of life. It was also one of the most expensive schools in the country, and his parents tried to change his mind because they could not afford it. However Jobs insisted that he would go to Reed College or nothing, and his parents eventually gave in.

Once at Reed College, though, Jobs was surprised to learn that despite the school's free-spirited reputation, it had a rigorous academic regimen that included numerous required courses. This was not the kind of education he wanted, and instead of following Reed's requirements, he only attended class when he felt like it and refused to take the courses that did not interest him. After six months he realized that he was wast-

The Power to Persuade

From the time that he was a boy, Jobs showed an amazing ability to persuade other people to believe what he wanted them to. Eric Schmidt, the executive chairman of Google, says, "He was so charismatic he could convince me of things I didn't actually believe." A fourth-grade teacher witnessed this power early in Jobs's life. She says that his school once held a Hawaii Day, when the students were supposed to dress up, but that Jobs did not wear the suggested Hawaiian shirt to school. However, she says, in the class photo he is wearing one because he was able to persuade another student to give him his shirt. Later, as part of the Hewlett-Packard Explorer's Club, Jobs decided to build a frequency counter—a device that measures the pulses per second in an electronic signal—but he did not have all the parts he needed. He called the CEO of Hewlett-Packard to ask for the parts. The CEO not only gave him the parts but also gave Steve a summer job at the plant where the company made frequency counters. Later, when Jobs worked at Atari, he used his powers of persuasion again when he managed to convince the company to pay some of the cost of his trip for spiritual enlightenment in India.

Eric Schmidt, as told to Jim Aley and Brad Wieners, "Eric Schmidt on Steve Jobs," *Bloomberg Businessweek Magazine*, October 6, 2011. www.businessweek.com.

ing his parents' hard-earned money, and he decided to drop out. However, he did not actually leave the school. Instead he obtained permission to audit classes and stayed with friends in the dorm. Jobs said, "I didn't have a dorm room, so I slept on the floor in friends' rooms, I returned coke bottles for the 5¢ deposits to buy food with, and I would walk the 7 miles across town every Sunday night to get one good meal a week at the Hare Krishna temple."[23]

Diversity of Experience

Auditing classes gave Jobs the freedom to learn about what interested him. He said, "Looking back it was one of the best decisions I ever made.

An ornate, new typeface is demonstrated. Jobs learned about typefaces, letter spacing, and font styles in a college calligraphy class—information he later put to use when he developed the Mac computer.

The minute I dropped out I could stop taking the required classes that didn't interest me, and begin dropping in on the ones that looked interesting." He believed this freedom to pursue whatever he wanted was greatly beneficial. He explained, "Much of what I stumbled into by following my curiosity and intuition turned out to be priceless later on."[24] One such class was calligraphy. In this class he learned about different styles of typefaces and spacing. He was impressed with the beauty of different writing styles, and he said this class was the inspiration for his later idea to create different typefaces on the Mac computer, a first in the world of computing, but something that every computer has today. He insisted, "If I had never dropped in on that single course in college, the Mac would have never had multiple typefaces or proportionately spaced fonts. And since Windows just copied Mac, it's likely that no personal computer would have them."[25]

Later in life Jobs spoke numerous times about the importance of pursuing diverse experiences throughout one's life, such as the calligraphy class he "dropped in on" in college. He explained that all of these experiences give a person the ability to do something he called "connecting the dots," which means drawing on all these experiences to create new things or ideas. He explained,

> Creativity is just connecting things. When you ask creative people how they did something, they feel a little guilty because they didn't really *do* it, they just *saw* something. It seemed obvious to them after a while. That's because they were able to connect experiences they've had and synthesize new things. And the reason they were able to do that was that they've had more experiences or they have thought more about their experiences than other people.[26]

He believed that people who do not have a broad enough life experience are less successful at coming up with creative ideas because they have fewer dots to connect.

Working at Atari

After his time at Reed College, Jobs worked as a technician for the video game manufacturer Atari. Atari produced Pong, which was one of the first arcade games. This two-player game digitally simulated Ping-Pong and was extremely popular. Atari later created the Atari Games Console, a platform for video game play that people could use at home by connecting it to their television. After seeing a help-wanted ad in the newspaper, Jobs landed his job at Atari by walking into the office and stating that he would not leave until the company hired him. Al Alcorn, chief engineer at the time, says, "I saw something in him. He was very intelligent, enthusiastic, excited about tech."[27] However, many of the other employees at Atari disagreed. In addition to being excited about technology, Jobs was often arrogant

"I saw something in him. He was very intelligent, enthusiastic, excited about tech."[27]

—Al Alcorn, former chief engineer at video game maker Atari.

and extremely critical of his coworkers. Furthermore, he had come to believe that because of his vegetarian diet, he had no body odor and did not need to shower, so he often smelled bad. Many of his coworkers wanted him to leave. Instead of firing him, however, his employer reduced the problem by moving him to the night shift, when fewer people would be around for him to interact with.

Quest for Enlightenment

At this time in his life Jobs was also very interested in spiritual enlightenment, and he traveled to India with his college friend Daniel Kottke. He even managed to convince Atari to cover some of the cost of the trip by making it part of a business trip. He traveled around India attending

While on a trip to India, Jobs attended religious festivals (similar to the one pictured) and met with Hindu gurus. Jobs had an interest in spiritual enlightenment but also a fascination with people whose actions had changed the world.

religious festivals and meeting various Hindu teachers, or gurus. He even had his head shaved. While in India Jobs also saw extreme poverty and suffering, and he began to wonder whether he might be able to do more to change the world through action rather than enlightenment. Jobs said, "It was one of the first times I started thinking that maybe [world-famous inventor] Thomas Edison did a lot more to improve the world than [philosopher] Karl Marx and [Indian guru] Neem Karoli Baba put together."[28] While Jobs did not abandon his search for spiritual enlightenment after his trip to India, when he returned to the United States he started to focus on changing the world through technology, as Thomas Edison had. Jobs and the technology company he helped start would ultimately have a significant impact on the world.

Chapter 2

Founding Apple Computer

According to the United States Census Bureau, in 2012, 78.9 percent of all US households had a computer. However, this was not the case when Steve Jobs was young. At that time computers were very large, expensive, and complicated. The first computers were so big they filled an entire room. Most early computers also required more than one person to operate them. Because they were so expensive and difficult to use, these early computers were typically owned only by large institutions such as universities.

However, in the early 1970s the technology company Intel developed the microprocessor, paving the way for significant changes in the computer industry. With the microprocessor, all the parts that make a computer think and function were placed on one small chip rather than many different parts. Intel says, "This revolutionary microprocessor, the size of a little fingernail, delivered the same computing power as the first electronic computer built in 1946, which filled an entire room."[29] As a result, it became possible to create a computer that was far smaller than before, and computers began to change dramatically.

The Homebrew Club

In 1975, when Jobs was twenty years old, *Popular Electronics* magazine showcased one of these smaller new computers in its cover story. The Altair 8800 was a kit that allowed hobbyists to build their own computer. The magazine called it the first "minicomputer," and it was about the size of a microwave oven. The Altair looked very different from what people think of as a computer today. Writer Karen Blumenthal says, "It didn't come with any other accessories—no screen, no keyboard, not even a way to talk to it. To use it, a hobbyist had to write a program, and even then, about all the Altair could do was blink back with the lights on the front of the box."[30] However, the Altair made people begin to think of many new possibilities in the field and generated a lot of attention among electronics hobbyists. Many hobbyists tried to develop their own kits or to develop components that could be used with computers such as the Altair to make them more useful.

In the area where Jobs and Steve Wozniak lived, a group of electronics hobbyists interested in computers created the Homebrew Computer

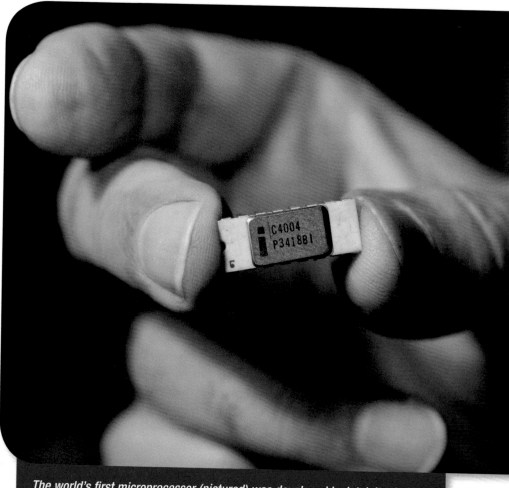

The world's first microprocessor (pictured) was developed by Intel. Its tiny size, not much larger than a fingernail, opened the way for small computers.

Club. It was a place for electronics enthusiasts to share their kits and knowledge about computers, and Jobs and Wozniak became members. Homebrew member Lee Felsenstein remembers that Jobs was extremely interested in computers even then. "What I remember is how intense he looked," says Felsenstein. "He was everywhere, and he seemed to be trying to hear everything people had to say."[31] Wozniak describes how inspired all the Homebrew members were about the future of computing. He says, "We were talking about a world—a possible world—where computers could be owned by anybody, used by anybody, no matter who you were or how much money you made. We wanted them to be affordable—and we wanted them to change people's lives."[32]

Even before the Altair was showcased in 1975, Wozniak had been working to create his own computer. He and a friend had already designed a very simple computer nicknamed the "cream soda computer" because they had been drinking a lot of cream soda while creating it. Like the Altair, it had no screen or keyboard and communicated information with blinking lights.

The First Apple Computer

However, when Wozniak saw the Altair's use of a microprocessor, he was inspired, and he had a vision about how to create a new type of computer. He says, "This whole vision of a personal computer just popped into my head."[33] Like the Altair this computer would use the new Intel chip. As a result it would be small enough to fit on a desktop. However, Wozniak's computer would be quite different from the Altair. Unlike the Altair computer, on which switches were used to enter data, Wozniak's computer would have a keyboard and screen connected to it. The user could enter commands on the keyboard and see those commands displayed on the screen. After months of work Wozniak tested his computer on June 29, 1975. "I typed a few keys on the keyboard and I was shocked! The letters were displayed on the screen!" he says. "It was the first time in history anyone had typed a character on a keyboard and seen it show up on the screen right in front of them."[34] Wozniak's invention became the first Apple computer.

A Productive Partnership

Steve Jobs and Steve Wozniak had very different personalities and priorities, but with these differences they created a partnership that yielded extraordinary results. Wozniak had the knowledge and skill to actually create the Apple computer. Jobs's more outgoing personality and drive to make money helped push them to financial success. In his memoir Wozniak stresses that the common perception that he and Jobs engineered the first Apple computers together is wrong. He says, "I did them alone." However, he also admits that Jobs played a key role in the success of the computers that he created. He says, "It never crossed my mind to sell computers. It was Steve who said, 'Let's hold them in the air and sell a few.'" In fact, Wozniak says, "Every time I'd design something great, Steve would find a way to make money for us." Walter Isaacson reports that after Wozniak created the Apple I his father confronted Jobs, charging that Jobs did not deserve half the profits because Wozniak was the one who created the computer. However, unlike his father Wozniak felt that their partnership was valuable and chose to remain partners with Jobs.

Steve Wozniak, with Gina Smith, *iWoz: Computer Geek to Cult Icon: How I Invented the Personal Computer, Co-Founded Apple, and Had Fun Doing It*. New York: W.W. Norton, 2006, p. 287.

Quoted in Walter Isaacson, *Steve Jobs*. Simon & Schuster: New York, 2011, p. 62.

Wozniak was happy to share his ideas with others for free. In fact, the Homebrew Club that he belonged to was based on the principle of sharing information rather than trying to make money from it, and Wozniak embraced that. He says, "I designed . . . [this first computer] because I wanted to give it away for free to other people."[35] However, Jobs saw things differently. He noticed that Wozniak's computer was extremely popular and suggested that rather than simply giving his designs away, the two go into business together and sell the product. Wozniak agreed, and they decided to create circuit boards—which are the heart of the computer—at a cost of twenty dollars and sell them for forty dollars. The buyers could assemble the other components—such as a keyboard and monitor—themselves. Wozniak remembers the excitement he and Jobs felt about starting their own company. He says, "We were in his car and he said—and I can remember him saying this like it was yesterday: 'Well, even if we lose our money, we'll have a company. For once in our lives, we'll have a company.'"[36]

The Creation of Apple Computer

In order to raise money to start their own company Jobs sold his Volkswagen van, and Wozniak sold his Hewlett-Packard calculator, and together they raised $1,300. Jobs had recently spent time working on an apple farm and suggested Apple for the company name. He said, "It sounded fun, spirited, and not intimidating. Apple took the edge off the word 'computer.'"[37] On April 1, 1976, they created Apple Computer. Wozniak and Jobs each received a 45 percent stake in the company.

Ron Wayne, a former boss from Atari, became a partner, too, receiving the remaining 10 percent share. Wayne's job was to create a logo for the company and to write the instruction manual for their computer. However, less than two weeks later Wayne backed out of the company. If he had stayed he would be a billionaire today, but Wayne says that at that time he was not ready for the risk that he saw in Jobs. He was older than Jobs and Wozniak and had already tried to start a slot-machine company and lost a lot of money when that failed. He says, "If Apple had failed, I would have had bruises on top of bruises. Steve Jobs was an absolute whirlwind and I had lost the energy you need to ride whirlwinds."[38]

"Steve Jobs was an absolute whirlwind."[38]

—Ron Wayne, a founder of Apple Computer.

Early Business

Apple's first business order was for Paul Terrell, who owned a computer store called the Byte Shop. Terrell says that at that time he already had too many computer kits. However, he saw that there was a need for fully assembled computers for all those people who wanted a computer but did not have the technical knowledge to assemble one. He says, "I

Steve Jobs (left) and Steve Wozniak (right) work on an early computer in 1976, the year they founded Apple Computer. To raise money to start the company, Jobs sold his VW van and Wozniak sold his Hewlett-Packard calculator.

needed an assembled and tested microcomputer that I could sell to all the programmers who were storming my stores for a taste of the hobby computer. In those days, if you didn't have an electronic technician buddy that could solder and troubleshoot the computer kits that were out there, you were out of luck."[39]

Jobs had what Terrell was looking for, and Terrell agreed to pay $500 for each computer, ordering fifty for a total of $25,000. Jobs, Wozniak, and various friends and family members including Jobs's sister Patty worked hard to complete the order, which had to be delivered within thirty days. They met their deadline; however, a misunderstanding between

The Apple Name

When Jobs and Wozniak created Apple Computers, there was already another well-known company with the Apple name: Apple Corps, which owns Apple Records, the Beatles' record label. According to Wozniak, when Jobs suggested the Apple name Wozniak's first concern was for a potential conflict with Apple Records. However, he says, "Steve didn't think Apple Records would have a problem since it was a totally different business." It turned out that Apple Records did have a problem with them using the Apple name, and there has been a long-running dispute between the two companies. In 1978 Apple Corps sued Apple Computer for trademark infringement. The lawsuit was eventually settled, with Apple Computer agreeing not to enter the music business. However, in 1986 Apple Corps charged that Apple Computer had violated the agreement by adding audio-recording features to its computers and sued again. A settlement was reached in 1991. Yet another lawsuit was launched by Apple Corps in 2003 after Apple Computers did enter the music business by releasing the iPod and opening the iTunes music store. In 2007, however, a judge ruled in favor of Jobs's company. Apple Inc. now owns all Apple trademarks and licenses some of them to Apple Corps.

Steve Wozniak, with Gina Smith, *iWoz: Computer Geek to Cult Icon: How I Invented the Personal Computer, Co-Founded Apple, and Had Fun Doing It.* New York: W.W. Norton, 2006, p. 174.

Apple and Terrell was discovered when they delivered their product. Terrell was expecting fifty fully assembled computers, including monitors and keyboards, but Jobs had created only fifty circuit boards. However, using his characteristic power to persuade, Jobs was able to convince Terrell to accept their product.

This first computer was called the Apple I. It was not geared toward the general public but toward computer hobbyists who knew how to program it. Jobs and Wozniak used their profits from Terrell's order to build more computers. Jobs said that while they did not sell very many of these first computers in total, the Apple I was important because it inspired them to see their company as a real business and to go on to create products that were successful. He said, "We sold only about 150 of them, ever. It wasn't that big a deal, but we made about $95,000 and I started to see it as a business besides something to do."[40] In 1976 they were even the subject of an article in the hobbyist magazine *Interface*, which made them feel even more like they had a real business.

The Apple II

In 1976 the first annual Personal Computer Festival was held in Atlantic City, New Jersey, and it would significantly influence the future of Apple Computer. Jobs and Wozniak attended with the Apple I. At that time Wozniak was already hard at work on the Apple II, a greatly improved new computer model. In fact, he spent most of his time in Atlantic City working on it in their hotel room. However, Jobs's attendance at the festival was also very important to the development of the Apple II. By this time Apple had a number of competitors, and these companies showcased their computers at the festival. While he was looking at the competition, Jobs had an important realization: that personal computers need to come in a complete package. "My vision was to create the first fully packaged computer," he said. "We were no longer aiming for the handful of hobbyists who liked to assemble their own computers, who knew how to buy transformers and keyboards. For every one of them there were a thousand people who would want the machine to be ready to run."[41] He also realized that not only should the computer be fully packaged, it needed to be polished and professional looking.

In order to produce this polished and professional computer, Wozniak and Jobs needed money. They managed to convince marketing specialist Mike Markkula to invest $250,000 in the company. In 1977 Apple Computer Inc. was created, with Jobs, Wozniak, and Markkula each having a third ownership. However, none of the three cofounders was president of their new company. Instead they brought in somebody with more experience; Michael Scott, a friend of Markkula's who had been the head of manufacturing at a company called National Semiconductor, became Apple's first chief executive officer (CEO). Jobs and Wozniak worked on developing Apple products, and Markkula was in charge of marketing. It was not until twenty years later that Jobs would become CEO of Apple.

In addition to providing the money that Apple needed, Markkula taught Jobs about marketing and sales, and his philosophies played a role in helping to guide how the new company would do business. When Apple Computer Inc. was created, Markkula wrote a paper called "The Apple Marketing Philosophy," which emphasizes the importance of presenting a product to the consumer in the right way. He says, "People DO judge a book by its cover. We may have the best product, the highest quality, the most useful software, etc.; if we present them in a slipshod manner, they will be perceived as slipshod; if we present them in a creative, professional manner, we will *impute* the desired qualities."[42] Markkula's philosophy is evident today in the way that Apple is known for not only producing beautiful products but also packaging them in a beautiful way. Jobs said, "When you open the box of an iPhone or iPad, we want that tactile experience to set the tone for how you perceive the product." He added, "Mike taught me that."[43]

> "We may have the best product, the highest quality, the most useful software, etc.; if we present them in a slipshod manner, they will be perceived as slipshod."[42]
>
> —Mike Markkula, a marketing specialist who owned a third of the fledgling Apple Computer.

Leading the Way for Other Computers

Unlike the Apple I, which was designed for people who knew a lot about electronics, the Apple II was designed with the average person in mind. It was ready to run right out of the box. It also had high-resolution color graphics—one of the first computers to have that feature—a built-in keyboard, speaker, and power supply. Jobs had very definite ideas about how he wanted the Apple II to look. Instead of a metal case like all the other computers, he had a beige-colored plastic case created. He also hired somebody to create a new type of power supply. Other computers at that time also contained a noisy fan, which was necessary to reduce the heat created by the power supply. However, Jobs did not like the noise fans created. He hired engineer Rod Holt to design a power supply that did not generate heat, thus eliminating the need for a fan. Finally, the

The Apple II computer (pictured) was considered by many to be a visionary idea of a personal computer. It was described at the time as far ahead of other computer designs.

Apple II had a new logo, a simple rainbow-colored Apple with a bite taken out of it (a play on the word *byte*). It sold for $1,298.

Most people agree that the Apple II was ahead of its time and led the way for other computer companies that followed. Wozniak says that his creation was far ahead of its competition. He says, "Other computers eventually caught up, but it took years for them to match what I'd done."[44] Journalist Harry McCracken agrees. He argues, "It was . . . easily the most visionary of the early personal computers—the one based on the clearest idea of what a PC should be, and where it could go." He adds,

"The Apple II readied the world for the Mac, the iPod, the iPhone, the iPad and, come to think of it, every other major technology gadget of the past 35 years. More than any single other computing device, it's the one that crawled out of the primordial ooze and scampered assertively in the right direction. Countless others followed its lead, and continue to do so."[45]

"The Apple II readied the world for the Mac, the iPod, the iPhone, the iPad and, come to think of it, every other major technology gadget of the past 35 years."[45]

—Harry McCracken, journalist.

Jobs and Wozniak had worked hard to achieve that success. In fact, throughout his life Jobs continually stressed the importance of hard work in business. He said, "I'm convinced that about half of what separates the successful entrepreneurs from the non-successful ones is pure perseverance. It is so hard. You put so much of your life into this thing. There are such rough moments in time that I think most people give up. I don't blame them. It is really tough and it consumes your life."[46]

Success of the Apple II

Jobs and Wozniak were rewarded for their hard work when they revealed the Apple II to the public at the West Coast Computer Faire in San Francisco in 1977. It was successful from the start. Within weeks of the show Apple had received three hundred orders, already surpassing total sales of the Apple I. By September 1978 sales had reached $7.9 million. The company moved into a real office in Cupertino. There was even a waiting list for the Apple II computer. Jobs was just twenty-three years old and part of a company that would soon be known throughout the world.

Chapter 3

Challenges

In 1980 Apple Computer decided that it had grown large and success-ful enough to become a public company. This means that owner-ship shares in Apple would be publicly traded on the New York Stock Exchange. Steve Jobs owned 15 percent of those shares, and at age twenty-five he suddenly became worth more than $200 million. Steve Wozniak sold and gave away some of his stock to others, but even then he was still worth millions of dollars, too. Wozniak remembers how much excitement was generated when Apple went public. He says, "It was the most successful IPO [initial public offering; the first sale of a company's shares to the public] up to that time. It was on the front page of every major newspaper and magazine. Suddenly we were legendary. And rich. Really rich."[47]

Not the Typical Millionaire Lifestyle

Despite being so rich, Jobs did not live the life of a typical millionaire. In an interview with Walter Isaacson, he explained his attitude about money. Jobs said that he had never been worried about money before he became rich—his parents had taken care of him growing up, and he had been voluntarily poor in college and been okay—so in a way, be-coming a millionaire did not change things a lot. Jobs said that he went from being poor and not worrying about money, to being rich and not worrying about money.

He also said that in addition to not focusing too much on money, he was determined not to let that money change him as he had seen it change others. He explained, "I watched people at Apple who made a lot of money and felt they had to live differently. Some of them bought a Rolls-Royce and various houses, each with a house manager and then someone to manage the house managers. Their wives got plastic surgery and turned into these bizarre people. This was not how I wanted to live. It's crazy. I made a promise to myself that I'm not going to let this money ruin my life."[48] Isaacson believes that Jobs was successful in his desire not to be changed by money. He observes, "The houses he lived in, no matter how rich he became, tended not to be ostentatious and were furnished so simply they would have put a Shaker to shame. Neither then nor later would he travel with an entourage, keep a personal staff, or even have security protection."[49] Those who visited Jobs's house often commented on how understated it was in comparison to how much money Jobs had. For example, in a 1997 interview he conducted at Jobs's house, journalist Steve Lohr described a comfortable and spacious red-brick home that he estimated to be worth about $3 million to $5 million. However, he observed, "For a man worth an estimated $700 million, the house seems a statement of restraint."[50]

> "I made a promise to myself that I'm not going to let this money ruin my life."[48]
>
> —Steve Jobs.

The Apple III and the Lisa

Jobs's company had gone public, making him a multimillionaire, and the Apple II continued to sell well. However, Jobs knew that the company could not keep going forever based on this one product. In order to remain successful it needed to keep creating innovative new products and stay ahead of its competition, but doing so proved to be a struggle. Apple's next two computers did not achieve the same level of success that the Apple II had. In fact, they were both failures.

The Apple III debuted in 1980. While the Apple II was designed for homes and schools, the Apple III was designed for businesses. Unfortunately, it had numerous technical problems. Wozniak describes it as a complete disaster. He says, "The Apple III had hardware problems, serious ones. It would get to a store, for instance, boot up a couple of times, and then it would crash. Sometimes it wouldn't even boot up at all." He adds,

My brother had a computer store by this time in Sunnyvale, and he told me Apple engineers would come down to fix it, but they could never get a machine that worked. Never. The first few months of the Apple III went by, and many of the stores had the same experience. Every Apple III came back not working. And what do you do when you're a computer dealer and this happens? Well, you stop selling it.[51]

As a result of its many problems, few people wanted to buy the Apple III, and sales were poor.

The Lisa computer debuted in 1983, and despite having some attractive features it was also a failure. The Lisa's most innovative feature was called a graphical interface system. While the Apple II required users to enter commands on the keyboard, with the Lisa, users

The Lisa computer (pictured), with its mouse that allowed a user to point and click on objects displayed on the computer screen, did not catch on with consumers. One problem was price; at $9,995, it was too expensive for the average person.

Graphical User Interface

The graphical user interface and mouse are standard features of computers today, but when Apple added them to the Lisa computer, they were an exciting new concept. Up until then, to get a computer to do something, a person typed a character on the keyboard, and that showed up on the monitor screen. A graphical user interface had pictures of things already on the screen, and a person simply used a mouse to point to the one they wanted and clicked on it. However, Apple did not invent this technology by itself. Instead, Jobs took the idea of a graphical user interface and the mouse from the Xerox Company. In 1979 he toured its Palo Alto Research Center and saw an experimental computer called the Alto, which had a three-button mouse and a graphical display. He said that he instantly recognized the value of what Xerox had. Later he remarked, "It was one of those sort of apocalyptic moments. I remember within ten minutes of seeing the graphical user interface stuff, just knowing that every computer would work this way some day; it was so obvious once you saw it. It didn't require tremendous intellect. It was so clear." Jobs immediately went back to Apple and had the engineers there create a mouse and graphical user interface for Apple, making it even better than the one Xerox was working on.

Steve Jobs, interview by Daniel Morrow, "Excerpts from an Oral History Interview with Steve Jobs," Smithsonian Institution, April 20, 2005. http://americanhistory.si.edu.

manipulated a mouse to point and click on objects that were displayed on the screen. The Lisa also had numerous software programs including a word processor, spreadsheets, and a drawing program. However, Jobs put millions of dollars into developing the Lisa, continually asking its engineers to add new features or change existing ones, and the project went far over budget. The Lisa cost so much money to develop that it ended up being priced at $9,995, which was too expensive for most people. This price tag meant that the Lisa was only affordable for businesses; however, it ran so slowly that it lost that market as well.

The Lisa was not a commercial success, and Jobs was removed from its team while development continued without him.

When the Apple II was released Apple was far ahead of its competitors, but by this time the company had begun working on new models like the Lisa and the Apple III, and it faced serious competition from other computer companies. One of its biggest competitors was International Business Machines (IBM). In 1981 IBM released a personal computer which sold for $1,565. While Jobs insisted that IBM's computer was inferior, sales were good. By the end of its first year IBM's share of the market was growing, while Apple's was not.

The Macintosh

After the failure of both the Apple III and the Lisa, Apple did have success with the Macintosh, or "Mac," computer. The development of this computer began without Jobs. While Jobs was working on the Lisa, another team at Apple was trying to create an affordable computer for the average person. Director of Publications and New Product Review Jef Raskin was leading the project, and he named the project Macintosh, an intentional misspelling of the name of his favorite apple, the McIntosh. He originally wanted it to sell for $1,000. However, after Jobs got taken off the Lisa team he went to the Macintosh team, where he quickly took over, and Raskin's dream of a low-cost computer quickly faded.

As he had done with the Lisa, Jobs kept insisting on adding various features to the computer, which increased the price. For example, he did not like the cheap microprocessor that Raskin had chosen and eventually forced the team to replace it with a better but more expensive one. Award-winning journalist Malcolm Gladwell talks about how Jobs obsessed over every detail on the Macintosh, wanting it to be perfect. For example, he says,

> he looked at the title bars—the headers that run across the top of windows and documents—that his team of software developers had designed for the original Macintosh and decided he didn't like them. He forced the developers to do another version, and then

another, about twenty iterations in all, insisting on one tiny tweak after another, and when the developers protested that they had better things to do he shouted, "Can you imagine looking at that every day? It's not just a little thing. It's something we have to do right."[52]

As a result of Jobs's desire for perfection, the price for the Macintosh ended up being $2,495, significantly higher than was originally planned.

There are differing opinions about the impact of Jobs taking over the Macintosh project. Raskin was not happy with the way Jobs handled the project or with the way he treated him. In a 1981 memo sent to Mike Scott, the president of Apple at that time, Raskin states that Jobs is a dreadful manager. He says, "Very often, when told of a new idea, he will immediately attack it and say that it is worthless or even stupid." However, he adds, "if the idea is a good one, [Jobs] will soon be telling people it as though it was his own."[53] Raskin and Jobs disagreed so much that Raskin eventually had to leave the Macintosh project. However, while Raskin and some others were critical of Jobs, others insist that despite his criticism and disregard for the feelings of others, Jobs had the unique creative vision and drive to succeed that the Macintosh team needed. Andy Hertzfeld was on the team that created the Macintosh, and he says that Jobs was a crucial part of its creation. He insists, "The Macintosh never would have happened without him, in anything like the form it did. Other individuals are responsible for the actual creative work, but Steve's vision, passion for excellence and sheer strength of will, not to mention his awesome powers of persuasion, drove the team to meet or exceed the impossible standards that we set for ourselves."[54]

> "Steve's vision, passion for excellence and sheer strength of will . . . drove the [Macintosh] team to meet or exceed the impossible standards that we set for ourselves."[54]
>
> —Andy Hertzfeld, former Apple employee.

Introducing the Mac to the World

With Jobs in control of the Macintosh project, Apple created a famous commercial for the 1984 Super Bowl to introduce the product to the public. It parodies the famous George Orwell novel *1984*, about a future in which the

Jobs shows off the first Macintosh, or Mac, computer. During the design stage Jobs made many changes to the computer, forcing Apple to raise its price.

government—headed by a shadowy leader known only as Big Brother—monitors and controls the population. In the commercial a woman with a sledgehammer is being chased by men in uniform. She runs into an auditorium filled with rows of workers who are watching a huge face that looks like Big Brother talking on a screen. She shatters the screen with the sledgehammer and a voice says, "On January 24th, Apple Computer will introduce Macintosh. And you'll see why 1984 won't be like '1984.'" Apple's message was that its competitor, IBM, was boring and controlling like Big Brother, but the Mac would break that control and bring new ideas into the computer world. The commercial successfully generated a large amount of public excitement about the upcoming computer release.

The Macintosh initially lived up to the hype generated by the 1984 commercial and sold very well. However, sales quickly began to dwindle.

The Desire for Perfection

Jobs was known for his obsessive attention to detail and his desire for perfection. While these attributes helped him create products that greatly appeal to the public, they also led to extreme frustration for many people who worked with him. Some complained that he took his desire for perfection too far and that it cost too much time and money. For example, when the case for the Apple II was designed, Jobs wanted it to be housed in a beige plastic shell. The company that Apple used for the shell had hundreds of shades of beige, but Jobs did not like any of them. Former Apple CEO Michael Scott says, "For all the standard colors of beige available in the world, of which there are thousands, none was exactly proper for him. So we actually had to create 'Apple beige' and get that registered." Scott says that Jobs also obsessed over the edges of the shell. He says, "Jobs wanted a rounded edge on it so it didn't have a hard feel. They spent weeks and weeks arguing exactly how rounded it would be."

Michael Scott, interview by Jay Yarrow, "XCLUSIVE: Interview with Apple's First CEO Michael Scott," *Business Insider*, May 24, 2011. www.businessinsider.com.

In reality, the Macintosh was slow and did not have enough power. In addition, it did not have a fan because Jobs did not like the noise fans made and had refused to put one in. The lack of a fan caused parts of the computer to fail. Some people even nicknamed it the beige toaster. Many people believed that the Macintosh's competition, the IBM PC, was cheaper and could do more. Because he had taken such a large role in the creation of the Mac, Jobs received a lot of the blame for its failure.

Tough Treatment of Other People

In addition to increasingly incurring blame for the business failures at Apple, Jobs was criticized for the way he treated coworkers and friends. Many people who worked with Jobs believed that he thought too much of himself; at the first company Halloween party he reinforced this perception by coming dressed in robes like Jesus Christ. Coworkers were not pleased with what they considered unprovoked rude behavior. Randy Wigginton worked as a programmer at Apple Computer in the early days. He says, "Steve would come in, take a quick look at what I had done, and tell me it was shit without having any idea what it was or why I had done it."[55] Wozniak says simply, "Steve was too tough on people."[56]

> "Steve was too tough on people."[56]
>
> —Steve Wozniak, cofounder of Apple Computer.

In many cases the recipients of this tough treatment did not even understand why they were being treated so harshly. For example, when Apple became a public company in 1980, high-level employees received the option to buy stock, and as a result, many became millionaires. However, Daniel Kottke, who had been Jobs's friend since high school and had worked for Apple since it had started in Jobs's garage, was not given any stock options. Kottke says he repeatedly tried to ask Jobs about the options, yet Jobs continually brushed him off. Rod Holt, who built the power supply for the Apple II, reportedly tried to change Jobs's mind, suggesting that they both give Kottke some of their options. He offered to match whatever Jobs gave, and Jobs responded by offering to give Kottke nothing. Kottke maintains that he does not understand why Jobs treated him this way.

Chrisann Brennan

In addition to being hard on his coworkers Jobs was very hard on Chris-ann Brennan. Jobs met Brennan when they were in high school, and they had an on-again, off-again relationship. After Apple Computer was created, Jobs moved out of his parents' house and into a home he rented and shared with friends. Brennan moved in, too, and soon afterward she became pregnant. Their relationship quickly deteriorated as Jobs refused to accept responsibility for the pregnancy and even denied that he was the father. According to friends, he simply decided he did not want to have a child and proceeded to shut the whole issue out of his mind. "He would not talk to me,"[57] says Brennan. Ironically, Jobs and Brennan were the same age that Jobs's birth parents had been when they had him.

After being ignored by Jobs, Brennan moved out. She gave birth to a girl—Lisa Nicole Brennan—in 1978. Jobs helped name the baby, then went back to work and continued to ignore both Lisa and her mother. However, he did later name the Lisa computer after his daughter. Jobs did not provide child support, so Brennan lived on welfare. Eventually, the county sued Jobs in order to have him take a paternity test. He would be legally obligated to pay child support if Lisa proved to be his child. The test showed a probability of 94.41 percent that he was the father, and Jobs began to pay the required child support but still refused to acknowledge publicly that the baby was his. It was not until later in life that he regretted his behavior. He says, "I wish I had handled it differently. I could not see myself as a father then, so I didn't face up to it. . . . If I could do it over, I would do a better job."[58]

The Decline of Apple

By 1985, after the failures of the Apple III and the Lisa and the mediocre sales of the Macintosh, Apple was not doing well financially. In 1985 the company had its first quarterly loss and had to lay off some of its employees. Jobs had been unsuccessful in his attempt to create a dazzling new computer that would match the popularity of the Apple II. In addition, his tensions with coworkers did not aid the company's progress. In 1983 Apple had hired John Sculley, former CEO of PepsiCo Inc., to become its new chief executive officer. Jobs was the one who recruited Sculley and pressured him to take the job. However, not long after Sculley agreed to come to work for Apple, he and Jobs began to disagree with one another, both insisting that the other should leave Apple.

In April 1985 Apple's board of directors decided to meet privately with both Sculley and Jobs in order to resolve the dispute. Hertzfeld remembers, "After long wrenching discussions with both of them, and extending

John Sculley (pictured) took over as Apple's chief executive officer in 1983. He and Jobs did not see eye-to-eye on the company's future direction; two years later the company's board of directors stripped Jobs of all authority with Apple.

the meeting to the following day, the board decided in favor of John, instructing him to reorganize the Macintosh division, stripping Steve of all authority. . . . For the time being, no operating role was defined for him."[59] Shortly after that, Sculley told a group of analysts that the company did not need Jobs. He said, "From an operations standpoint, there is no role either today or in the future for Steve Jobs."[60] At thirty years old, Jobs was left in the unenviable position of being unwanted in the company that he had started nine years earlier.

Time Away from Apple

By 1985 Apple had taken Jobs off all its projects. As chairman of the board he had no real job responsibilities. He was even moved to a new office that was so far away from the day-to-day operation of the company that it was nicknamed "Siberia," after a part of Russia that is famous for being so remote. In 1985 Jobs decided to resign. In his resignation letter he said, "The company's recent reorganization left me with no work to do and no access to regular management reports. I am but 30 and want still to contribute and achieve."[61]

He later realized that leaving Apple was a good thing for him, and it helped him re-spark his creativity. He said, "It turned out that getting fired from Apple was the best thing that could have ever happened to me. The heaviness of being successful was replaced by the lightness of being a beginner again, less sure about everything. It freed me to enter one of the most creative periods of my life."[62] However, Jobs was not immediately successful in his new endeavors, and at the time leaving Apple did not feel like the best thing that could ever have happened to him. In describing the way he felt about leaving Apple, he said, "You've probably had somebody punch you in the stomach and it knocks the wind out of you and you can't breathe."[63]

NeXT

Even though he no longer had a place at Apple, Jobs still wanted to create computers. He had been talking to academics about their computer needs and decided to create a computer that was specifically for scientists and people who worked in higher education. The computer would help with the time-consuming data evaluation that these people have to do. He also wanted to make it possible for these academics to link their computers together—or network them—in order to make it easy to share files and data.

Jobs shared his ideas with some of the people with whom he had worked at Apple, and five of them left the company to join him in founding a new company that they would call NeXT. In an interview right after his resignation Jobs expressed his belief that this small group of people would be successful in their new endeavor. He said, "We've all known each other for four years. And we have an immense amount of confidence in each others' abilities and genuinely like each other. And all have a desire to have a small company where we can influence its destiny and have a really fun place to work."[64] However, Apple was not happy with Jobs for pirating away employees it considered to be important to the company. Sculley argued that their inside knowledge would give Jobs an advantage in competing with Apple. Apple thus sued Jobs for taking its trade secrets. Jobs brushed off their concerns as completely overblown, saying, "It is hard to think that a $2 billion company with 4,300-plus people couldn't compete with six people in blue jeans."[65] The two groups eventually settled the lawsuit after Jobs agreed that his new company would focus on a different market. In order to finance his new venture, Jobs sold his Apple shares, receiving more than $100 million. He kept one share so that he could still attend Apple board meetings if he wanted to.

Disappointing Sales

NeXT was not as successful as Jobs had hoped. In fact, it was not a profitable company at all. A huge amount of money went into developing the NeXT computer, and the price reflected that. As in the past, Jobs's pursuit of perfection ended up blowing both budgets and deadline. For example, he insisted that the computer be in the shape of a cube. This made it more difficult and expensive to manufacture. Most existing computer parts were made to fit inside a larger case that was a rectangular shape. When the NeXT computer finally went on sale in 1989, long after its initial 1987 deadline, it cost $6,500. The optional printer was an extra $2,000, and the purchase of an external hard drive, which was advised,

In 1988 Steve Jobs talks to the media about his new company, NeXT. Jobs started NeXT after resigning from Apple in 1985.

added another $2,500 to the total bill. This was far too expensive for most academics. Jobs only sold about fifty thousand NeXT computers in total. Jeff Goodell says, "At NeXT, Jobs succeeded in producing a strikingly distinctive object—but one that proved way too expensive for the market. Consumers who bought NeXT computers still swoon over them, calling them the most beautiful machines ever built—but in the real world, nobody wanted to pay 10 grand for a beautiful machine."[66]

The NeXT Computer and the World Wide Web

While Jobs was not able to make NeXT commercially successful, many aspects of the computer were later recognized to be ahead of its peers from other companies. For example, in 1989 computer scientist Tim Berners-Lee used a NeXT computer to create the world's first web server and web

The Challenge of Furnishing a House

Jobs's insistence on not accepting anything less than perfection influenced the way he furnished his home. Visitors to his house noticed that because it was so difficult for him to find furniture that he liked, his house was very empty. For example, former Apple CEO John Sculley says, "I remember going into Steve's house and he had almost no furniture in it. He just had a picture of Einstein, whom he admired greatly, and he had a Tiffany lamp and a chair and a bed." Later, when he married and had a family, Jobs was forced to buy more household items; however, it was often a difficult process. For example, he talked about the process of buying a new washing machine. He says, "We spent some time in our family talking about what's the trade-off we want to make. We ended up talking a lot about design, but also about the values of our family. Did we care most about getting our wash done in an hour versus an hour and a half? Or did we care most about our clothes feeling really soft and lasting longer? Did we care about using a quarter of the water?" Jobs said, "We spent about two weeks talking about this every night at the dinner table." Finally, says Jobs, they decided on Miele appliances, which are made in Germany, and which he considered to be extremely well made and well designed, and to do the best job of washing clothes and conserving water.

John Sculley, interview by Leander Kahney, "John Sculley on Steve Jobs, the Full Interview Transcript," Cult of Mac, October 14, 2010. www.cultofmac.com.

Steve Jobs, interview by Gary Wolf, "Steve Jobs: The Next Insanely Great Thing," *Wired*, February 1996. http://archive.wired.com.

browser, which would become the foundation of the Internet. Berners-Lee says that the NeXT computer was an important part of his success. He says, "I wrote the program using a NeXT computer. This had the advantage that there were some great tools available—it was a great computing environment in general. In fact, I could do in a couple of months what would take more like a year on other platforms, because on the NeXT, a lot of it was done for me already."[67]

Pixar

In addition to starting NeXT, Jobs also purchased a computer animation studio called the Graphics Group from *Star Wars* creator George Lucas. He renamed it Pixar. At that time animated films were hand-drawn. A full-length animated film required hundreds of thousands of frames that had to be drawn and colored by hand, and this could take hundreds of hours. Pixar had a powerful animation computer that did the same thing automatically, eliminating many hours of work. Not only did the company's computer animation program save time and money, it also allowed more sophisticated images. Yet despite this potential, the company was not successful when Jobs purchased it. It was losing money and continued to do so after Jobs bought it and renamed it. He had to keep investing more and more to keep it going.

Jobs was initially interested in Pixar only for its computer, which he planned to sell to other industries that needed sophisticated imaging, such as hospitals. However, he realized that this would not work because the computer was too complicated for most people to operate. Pixar's success eventually came not by selling its technology but by making films.

John Lasseter, head of the animation department at Pixar, was the most important person in achieving this success. He created a short animated film called *Tin Toy* about a tin one-man-band toy that tries to escape from a destructive baby. The film won an Academy Award in 1989; it was the first computer-animated film to win one. After that, people began to pay more attention to the potential of computer animation. Impressed with *Tin Toy*, Disney asked Lasseter to create an animated film about toys, and he created *Toy Story*, the first full-length movie made with all computer-generated animation. *Toy Story* was released in 1995. It was extremely successful, making millions of dollars, and was followed by two sequels that were also successful. It had taken almost ten years of sticking with Pixar and investing money, but when *Toy Story* was released, Jobs finally received

> "I could do in a couple of months what would take more like a year on other platforms, because on the NeXT, a lot of it was done for me already."[67]
>
> —Tim Berners-Lee, creator of the World Wide Web.

public acknowledgment for his belief in computer-animated technology. He subsequently made Pixar into a public company and his stock was worth $1.2 billion.

Doing the Job Right

Lasseter says that he was greatly influenced by Jobs's philosophy of always making the very best product he could. He says, "Early on when I was making 'Toy Story' we started talking and he said, 'John, you know at Apple when I make computers, what is the lifespan of this product, two years, three years at the most, and then about five years, they're like a doorstop. But if you do your job right, these films can last forever.' I was amazed by that statement, and I was humbled by it too." He says, "It really affected me in terms of understanding the potential of animation, and if we do our job right, meaning: tell a great story with really memorable characters and make it beautiful and make it great. If you can do that then these films will entertain audiences for generations."[68]

> "[What Jobs said] really affected me in terms of understanding the potential of animation, and if we do our job right . . . then these films will entertain audiences for generations."[68]
>
> —John Lasseter, chief creative officer at Pixar.

In addition to encouraging Lasseter to strive for perfection, Jobs persevered with Pixar because he believed that it had value. He did this even when other people did not agree with him, and the company lost money year after year. Sticking to his beliefs no matter what was one of the reasons Jobs was so successful in his life. He explained this philosophy in a famous 2005 commencement address he gave at Stanford University. He said, "Your time is limited, so don't waste it living someone else's life. Don't be trapped by dogma—which is living with the results of other people's thinking. Don't let the noise of others' opinions drown out your own inner voice. And most important, have the courage to follow your heart and intuition. They somehow already know what you truly want to become."[69]

Laurene Powell

In 1989, while he was trying to make NeXT and Pixar successful, Jobs met Laurene Powell, the woman he would marry. She was an MBA stu-

John Lasseter, the computer animation genius behind Pixar and Toy Story, was impressed by Jobs's philosophy of always making the best products possible. Jobs's belief in computer-animation technology helped make Pixar a success.

dent at Stanford University where Jobs was giving a class talk. After the class the two exchanged business cards, then Jobs had to leave for a business meeting. Jobs remembered, "I was in the parking lot, with the key in the car, and I thought to myself, If this is my last night on earth, would I rather spend it at a business meeting or with this woman? I ran

Complete Confidence in His Ability

Part of the reason that Jobs was so successful in his career was that when he decided to do something, he believed with certainty that he would be successful. Eric Schmidt, the executive chairman of Google, talks about how Jobs came back to Apple in 1997 when it was on the brink of collapse, confident that he could make it successful again, and he did. Schmidt says, "I had no clue how to do what he did. When somebody tells you they're going to do something and you say, 'I don't understand how you're going to do that,' and they succeed? That is the ultimate humbling experience." Jobs managed to do this again and again throughout his life. Schmidt talks about how Jobs developed the iPad. He says, "When he started working on tablets, I said nobody really likes tablets. The tablets that existed were just not very good." Steve said: "No, we *can* build one." And he did. In 2010 Apple released a tablet computer that it named the iPad, and it has remained extremely successful.

Eric Schmidt, as told to Jim Aley and Brad Wieners, "Eric Schmidt on Steve Jobs," *Bloomberg Businessweek Magazine*, October 6, 2011. www.businessweek.com.

across the parking lot, asked her if she'd have dinner with me. She said yes, we walked into town and we've been together ever since."[70] His biological sister, Mona, recalls, "I remember when he phoned the day he met Laurene. 'There's this beautiful woman and she's really smart and she has this dog and I'm going to marry her.'"[71] Like Jobs, Powell was a vegetarian, was interested in Zen Buddhism, and was very intelligent.

Yet even in his relationship with Powell, Jobs was difficult at times. Walter Isaacson says that while Jobs was extremely focused and affectionate some of the time, at other times he ignored Powell. For instance, Jobs proposed to her in 1990, then did not mention or act on the proposal for months. Powell got sick of waiting for him to make up his mind and moved out. Then Jobs gave her an engagement ring, and she moved back in. The two took a trip to Hawaii, and she became pregnant. However, according to Isaacson, even after Powell was pregnant Jobs was not sure about getting married, and she moved out again. He finally did make up his mind, though, and the two were married in 1991 at the Ahwahnee Lodge in Yosemite National Park. Their wedding cake was made in the shape of the famous Half Dome rock, and the guests all went hiking after the wedding.

Jobs and Powell had three children together: Reed Powell, Erin Sienna, and Eve. In addition, his daughter Lisa came to live with the new family and finally had the opportunity to establish a real relationship with her father. While Jobs had not been a good father in the early part of Lisa's life, he became more involved as he grew older. His sister

Laurene Powell (pictured in 2013) and Steve Jobs married in 1991. The couple had three children together, and Jobs's daughter from a previous relationship came to live with the family.

Mona says that he was extremely interested in all his children. She says, "When Reed was born, he began gushing and never stopped. He was a physical dad, with each of his children. He fretted over Lisa's boyfriends and Erin's travel and skirt lengths and Eve's safety around the horses she adored."[72] Yet, while Jobs clearly loved his children, the fact was that work consumed a large part of his life. According to Isaacson, Jobs's daughter Erin asked to be interviewed for her father's biography and told him, "Sometimes I wish I had more of his attention, but I know the work he's doing is very important."[73] Jobs also recognized that his work sometimes came before family. In fact, in their final interview he told Isaacson that one of the reasons he wanted the biography written was so that his children would know him and understand why he was not always there for them.

The Importance of Failure

When he left Apple and struggled with NeXT and Pixar, many people said that Jobs was a failure. But as Jobs's experience shows, failure can actually be an important part of becoming successful. Jobs explained this in his 2005 commencement address to the graduating class of Stanford University. Sheena Chestnut Greitens was one of the graduates Jobs spoke to that day. She explains, "What I learned that day, and in the years after graduation, is that contrary to what we've been often told, it's not just OK to fail. It's essential."[74] She explains that Jobs helped her realize that the fear of failure often stops people from trying, but the trying is what is essential because it is what ultimately leads to success. As a result, she says, sometimes failure is an opportunity in disguise. When a person has already failed, that fear of failing is gone, and he or she is free to pursue what they are passionate about. Jobs's failure at Apple left him free to pursue new ventures such as NeXT and Pixar, and through these experiences he became ready to return to Apple and lead them to success once again.

"What I learned that day [from Jobs], and in the years after graduation, is that contrary to what we've been often told, it's not just OK to fail. It's essential."[74]

—Sheena Chestnut Greitens, member of the 2005 Stanford University graduating class.

A Historic Comeback

By 1996 Apple was struggling and in need of new leadership. It also needed a new operating system for its computers. These two factors gave Jobs his opportunity to return to the company he loved. While NeXT computers were not very popular, it is widely recognized that they did have a powerful operating system, NeXTSTEP. Jobs persuaded Apple that NeXTSTEP would be a good choice for its new operating system. In 1996 Apple purchased NeXT. Part of the deal included Jobs coming back to the company as a special adviser. Now Apple had a chance to recover, and Jobs was back at the company that had forced him to leave eleven years before.

Chapter 5

A Legacy of Innovation and Success

Many people, including Jobs himself, believe that he returned to Apple just in time to save it. When he came back as interim CEO in 1997 the company was experiencing huge losses. Jobs said, "Apple was about ninety days from going bankrupt back then. It was much worse than I thought."[75] Former CEO John Sculley agrees with Jobs's assessment. He says, "I'm actually convinced that if Steve hadn't come back when he did—if they had waited another six months—Apple would have been history. It would have been gone, absolutely gone."[76] Jobs immediately made a number of changes to the company, including laying off many employees and shutting down product lines that he did not like. He then started work on creating products that would bring the company back to a leadership position in the field of technology. In 2000 he became permanent CEO.

Not only did Jobs stop Apple from going bankrupt, he quickly helped the company become extremely successful and influential. With Jobs as its leader, Apple enjoyed success after success with products such as the iPod, the iPhone, and the iPad. These products not only earned billions of dollars for Apple, but they led the way for other companies and transformed the music, entertainment, and communications industries.

The iMac

After he returned to Apple, the first successful product that Jobs launched was the iMac. The iMac was a desktop computer designed to be portable and easy to use. Buyers could take it out of the box, plug it in, and use it immediately. It also had a handle so it could be easily carried. The iMac looked very different than any other computer that existed at that time; the screen and the body of the computer were inside a colorful see-through plastic case, which came in many different colors including Strawberry, Lime, Tangerine, and Sage.

In addition to being visually appealing, the iMac was designed to cater to a new and increasingly popular desire that people had to connect to the Internet. In fact, the *i* in *iMac* stood for *Internet*. At that time going online was a relatively new phenomenon, and while a lot of people wanted to do so, many did not have the necessary computer equipment or knowledge. The iMac was for these consumers. It would make it easy for them to get online. The iMac sold well from the beginning, and its success put Apple back as a leader in the industry.

> "I'm actually convinced that if Steve hadn't come back when he did . . . Apple would have been history. It would have been gone, absolutely gone."[76]
>
> —John Sculley, former CEO of Apple.

A Revolution in Music

After proving that Apple could still be an innovator in the computer industry, Jobs went on to create new products that would transform the music industry. Until then, CDs were the most common way to buy and listen to music. If a person wanted a portable source of music—for example, while going on a walk—he or she could use a small CD player. However, these portable disc players had flaws; they were still relatively bulky and were known for skipping parts of a song if they were jostled around too vigorously. It was possible to store music files and play them on a computer by converting them into a type of digital file called an MP3. However, there were no popular portable MP3 music players.

Apple changed that in 2001 with its release of the iPod, a portable device that can store and play music that is downloaded from a computer. Apple iPod users can organize their music on the computer with a program called iTunes, which serves as a library, a jukebox, and a storefront for music. The first iPods could store up to one thousand songs, yet they weighed only 6.5 ounces and could easily fit in a person's pocket. They could play up to ten hours before they needed to be recharged, and they sold for $399. Jobs said, "With iPod, listening to music will never be the same again."[77] He was right; iPods were a revolution in portable music. Fewer and fewer people purchased physical CDs, preferring to download music and carry music around with them on the iPod or other types of portable digital music players that followed in the iPod's footsteps.

iTunes Music Store

As it became more popular to store music on computers in MP3 files, however, illegal music sharing proliferated around the world. A music album is the property of those who create it and is only intended to be used by the person who purchases it. However, some people figured out how to create websites on which they could share their MP3 files for free with hundreds of other computer users. One of the biggest music-sharing websites was called Napster, and it was started in 1998 by college student Shawn Fanning. Music sharing through sites like Napster was illegal because the music companies and artists were not being paid for the music files that were being distributed for free. However, it was extremely difficult to stop such sharing. According to author Patricia Lakin, "At the height of its popularity, more than sixty million people worldwide used Napster, and it was obvious that digital downloads were the new and future way to distribute music."[78] This new form of distribution was causing music companies to lose money, and they found it very difficult to stop what was happening. A federal court ordered Napster to be shut down, but other, similar sites quickly sprang up.

In 2003 Apple helped stop this proliferation of illegal music sharing by opening the iTunes Music Store, where customers can download songs to their computers and iPods legally. iTunes customers can purchase entire albums for varying prices or simply choose single songs for ninety-nine cents each. Download and purchase are easy. Users also have the ability to preview thirty seconds of songs for free. Jobs persuaded the five major music companies to agree to let Apple sell their music through this online store. Apple technology prevents users from illegally sharing those songs with other people. The ease and variety of the music offered in the iTunes store greatly reduced illegal music sharing.

Against the backdrop of the now-iconic iPod commercial, Steve Jobs introduces a new version of the iPod digital music player in 2004. The iPod's original release in 2001 marked a huge change in music buying and listening habits.

iPhone

The iPod was extremely successful, but Jobs did not stop there. In 2007, under his leadership, Apple released the iPhone, a touch-screen telephone and minicomputer that revolutionized the entire concept of the cell phone. In addition to being used for phone calls, texting, and e-mail,

Apple Products in Schools

Today many students use iPads or other Apple products in school. Jobs spoke about how he worked hard to help make this happen. In 1995, when many students did not have computers in their schools, he said, "I thought if there was just one computer in every school, some of the kids would find it. It will change their life." However, he realized that for many children this was not happening. He said, "We realized that a whole generation of kids was going to go through the school before they even got their first computer so we thought *the kids can't wait*. We wanted to donate a computer to every school in America." Jobs said that due to politics, this did not happen. However, in the 1980s the company did give away thousands of computers to schools in California. Despite such efforts, Jobs was also quick to point out that computers are not the most important part of education. He argued, "The elements of discovery are all around you. You don't need a computer." Instead, he insisted that the most important thing is a teacher who can inspire and incite curiosity.

Steve Jobs, interview by Daniel Morrow, "Excerpts from an Oral History Interview with Steve Jobs," Smithsonian Institution, April 20, 1995. http://americanhistory.si.edu.

the iPhone allows people to access the Internet and download music, movies, and videos. They can also sync data such as contacts and calendars with a computer. When Jobs introduced the iPhone in 2007, he emphasized this amazing versatility. He said,

> Well today, we're introducing THREE revolutionary new products. The first one is a widescreen iPod with touch controls. The second is a revolutionary new mobile phone. And the third is a breakthrough internet communications device. An iPod, a phone, an internet mobile communicator. An iPod, a phone, an internet mobile communicator. . . . these are NOT three separate devices! And we are calling it iPhone![79]

He went on to use the iPhone to find and call the nearest Starbucks; then as a joke he ordered four thousand lattes to go. The iPhone initially sold for $499. Even at this high price it was successful. Today the iPhone faces competition from other smartphone manufacturers, but research shows that it still has a large share of the market; according to research company comScore, in 2014 about 40 percent of US smartphone subscribers owned an Apple phone.

iPad

Apple's next revolutionary product was the iPad, released in 2010. The iPad is a tablet computer with no keyboard, mouse, or external wires. It uses the same touch-screen technology as the iPhone, and like the iPhone it has been very successful. When he presented the iPad to the public, Jobs called it a truly magical and revolutionary product. "What this device does is extraordinary," he said. "It is the best browsing experience you've ever had. . . . It's unbelievably great . . . way better than a laptop. Way better than a smartphone."[80] The public agreed. According to Apple, the company sold over three hundred thousand iPads in the first day alone. Just twenty-eight days after introducing the iPad, it had sold 1 million of them. The popularity of iPads has helped Apple rise to a position of dominance in the computer industry. According to journalist Fred Vogelstein, "If you include iPad sales with those for desktops and laptops, Apple is now the largest P.C. maker in the world." He says, "Around 200 million iPhones and iPads were sold last year [2013], or more than twice the number of cars sold worldwide."[81]

> "Around 200 million iPhones and iPads were sold last year [2013], or more than twice the number of cars sold worldwide."[81]
>
> —Fred Vogelstein, journalist.

Generating Public Excitement

Part of the reason Apple's new products instantly became successful was Jobs's ability to excite the public about Apple technology. He was famous for his spectacular product launches, breaking months of extreme secrecy with a dramatic and exciting presentation in which he revealed

Apple's newest device. For example, in 1984, when the Macintosh computer debuted, he unveiled it onstage; then, after showing some of its features, he said that he would like to let the Macintosh speak for itself. Jobs pushed a button, and the Macintosh said, "Hello. I'm Macintosh. It sure is great to get out of that bag." This was unlike anything his audience had ever seen, and they went wild with applause.

Jobs also created public excitement about Apple products through Apple stores. These stores help introduce people to Apple products and

Consumers try out some of the many popular Apple products at one of the company's stores. Following new-product launches, Apple stores are often filled to capacity with eager buyers.

give Apple control over the way this is done. Apple opened its first stores in 2001 in Virginia and California. Apple stores are designed to invite people to come inside and try out various Apple products, hopefully finding something they want to buy. Apple explains,

> The computers on display in an Apple store aren't some type of artificial display—they're hooked up to video camcorders, digital cameras, iPods, music keyboards, etc. so the visitor can actually *create* something, burn it to a CD/DVD, and get a feel for the hardware and software. You can also access the Web, download e-mail or otherwise use the Web through the store's open Airport wireless system, and their heavy-duty data line.[82]

Stores are staffed by well-trained experts who can answer questions about Apple products. The creation of Apple stores has been successful in increasing sales. According to Apple, in 2012 there were 372 million visitors to Apple stores, and store sales totaled approximately 12 percent of the company's overall sales. Apple has opened more than four hundred stores in the United States. It also has stores in more than ten other countries.

Fighting Cancer

In 2003, in the midst of all this success at Apple, Jobs received some bad news. Doctors discovered that he had pancreatic cancer. Initially Jobs said that he was told to go home and get his affairs in order, which meant that he had just months to live. However, further tests revealed that the cancer was a slower-growing type that might be treated successfully, and doctors recommended surgery. Yet despite doctors' recommendations and the urging of his family, Jobs initially refused surgery, trying natural healing diets and cleansings instead. Walter Isaacson believes that Jobs thought he could successfully defeat the cancer, just as he had successfully overcome many other obstacles in his life. He says, "In the past he had been rewarded for what his wife called his 'magical thinking'—his assumption that he could will things to be as he wanted. But cancer does not work that way. . . . In July 2004 a CAT scan showed that the tumor had grown and possibly spread. It forced him to face reality."[83]

In 2004 Jobs realized that he could not will the cancer away, and he had surgery to remove it. Publicly, he claimed to be cured. In a 2005 speech he said, "I had the surgery and I'm fine now. That was the closest I've been to facing death, and I hope it's the closest I get for a few more decades."[84] In reality though, the cancer had spread. As Jobs worked hard at Apple to help create innovative new products such as the iPad, he also worked hard to fight the cancer that threatened his life. He lost a lot of weight and, despite his insistence that he was not sick, by 2008 there was widespread public speculation that he was unwell. In 2009 he continued to downplay his illness, blaming the weight loss on a hormone imbalance; however, shortly afterward his poor health forced him to take a medical leave. That year he received a liver transplant. However, even that was not enough to heal him.

In August 2011 Jobs's poor health forced him to resign as Apple's CEO. In his resignation letter he said, "I have always said if there ever came a day when I could no longer meet my duties and expectations as Apple's CEO, I would be the first to let you know. Unfortunately, that day has come."[85] Tim Cook, who had had joined Apple in 1998 and had been working as its chief operating officer, became the new CEO. In a 2014 interview Cook explains that even three years later he has left Jobs's office untouched. "It felt right to leave it as it is," he says. "That's Steve's office."[86]

Jobs's Death

Jobs died on October 5, 2011. In a eulogy for her brother, Mona Simpson says that Jobs retained both his determination and his appreciation for beauty to the very end of his life. She says that when he said good-bye to her, he told her that he was going to a better place, and she believes that in his last few moments of life he was working hard to get there.

Receiving a Liver Transplant

In the United States not enough organs are donated to meet the needs of the sick. According to the American Liver Foundation, more than sixteen thousand Americans are on the waiting list for a liver transplant. Unfortunately, some die before they receive the liver they need. Organ waiting lists operate according to very strict criteria, including a person's place on the list, how sick they are, and whether they are a good match for available organs. It is not possible to get preferential treatment simply because a person is rich or famous. However, it does seem that Jobs was able to receive his liver transplant more quickly than the average person because of his significant financial resources. There are multiple organ waiting lists across the United States, and this is where having money can help. CNN writer Ray Hainer explains, "Nothing prevents someone from being evaluated and listed at multiple transplant centers. As long as a patient has the wherewithal to fly around the country—and be available at the drop of a hat if a liver becomes available (this is when the private jet comes in handy)—a patient can, in theory, be evaluated by all the transplant centers in the country." In Jobs's case, he was on the organ waiting list in Tennessee, which has a far shorter waiting list than in California where he lived, and because of his wealth he was able to quickly travel there to receive his transplant when a liver became available.

Ray Hainer, "Did Steve Jobs' Money Buy Him a Faster Liver Transplant?," CNN, June 24, 2009. www.cnn .com.

She explains, "His breathing changed. It became severe, deliberate, purposeful." She says, "His breath indicated an arduous journey, some steep path, altitude. He seemed to be climbing. But with that will, that work ethic, that strength, there was also sweet Steve's capacity for wonderment, the artist's belief in the ideal, the still more beautiful later. . . . Steve's final words were: OH WOW. OH WOW. OH WOW."[87]

Steve Jobs, 56, died on October 5, 2011 as a result of complications caused by pancreatic cancer. Memorials like this one in London were erected at Apple stores worldwide.

A Lasting Impact on Society

Jobs forever transformed the world of technology. Following his death, Apple's board of directors released a statement that said, "Steve's brilliance, passion and energy were the source of countless innovations that enrich and improve all of our lives. The world is immeasurably better because of Steve."[88] These sentiments were echoed by countless other people who grieved the loss of a man who always strove to make an amazing product that would change people's lives. Jeff Goodell remembers an interview with Jobs shortly after Jobs had been diagnosed with pancreatic cancer. He shares his most poignant memory from that interview: "What I remember is this: Jobs leaning forward at the end of the table and looking at me directly, his eyes intense. 'I think that life is something that happens in a flash,' he said. He snapped his fingers. 'We just have a brief moment here, and then we are gone.'"[89] Jobs's moment on Earth was briefer than many other people get—he was just fifty-six years old when he died—yet his life has had a significant and lasting impact on society.

> "Steve's brilliance, passion and energy were the source of countless innovations that enrich and improve all of our lives. The world is immeasurably better because of Steve."[88]
>
> —The Apple board of directors.

Source Notes

Introduction: Steve Jobs and the Digital Age

1. Quoted in *Guardian*, "Tributes to Steve Jobs," October 5, 2011. www.theguardian.com.

2. Steve Jobs, interview by David Sheff, "Playboy Interview: Steve Jobs," *Playboy*, February 1985. http://longform.org.

3. Jeff Goodell, "The Steve Jobs Nobody Knew," *Rolling Stone*, October 27, 2011. www.rollingstone.com.

4. Quoted in Walter Isaacson, *Steve Jobs*. New York: Simon & Schuster, 2011, p. xx.

5. Quoted in *Guardian*, "Tributes to Steve Jobs."

6. Quoted in Isaacson, *Steve Jobs*, p. 567.

Chapter One: Early Life

7. Quoted in Isaacson, *Steve Jobs*, p. 5.

8. Quoted in Isaacson, *Steve Jobs*, p. 5.

9. Steve Jobs, interview by Daniel Morrow, "Excerpts from an Oral History Interview with Steve Jobs," Smithsonian Institution, April 20, 2005. http://americanhistory.si.edu.

10. Quoted in Isaacson, *Steve Jobs*, p. 6.

11. Quoted in Karen Blumenthal, *Steve Jobs: The Man Who Thought Different*. New York: Feiwel and Friends, 2012, p. 10.

12. Jobs, interview by Morrow, "Excerpts from an Oral History Interview."

13. Quoted in Isaacson, *Steve Jobs*, p. 12.

14. Jobs, interview by Morrow, "Excerpts from an Oral History Interview."

15. Quoted in Isaacson, *Steve Jobs*, p. 12.

16. Jobs, interview by Morrow, "Excerpts from an Oral History Interview."

17. Isaacson, *Steve Jobs*, p. 13.

18. Quoted in Goodell, "The Steve Jobs Nobody Knew."

19. Quoted in Isaacson, *Steve Jobs*, p. 25.

20. Quoted in Isaacson, *Steve Jobs*, p. 30.

21. Goodell, "The Steve Jobs Nobody Knew."

22. Quoted in Isaacson, *Steve Jobs*, p. 17.

23. Steve Jobs, commencement address, Stanford University, June 12, 2005.

24. Jobs, commencement address, Stanford University.

25. Quoted in Isaacson, *Steve Jobs*, p. 41.

26. Steve Jobs, interview by Gary Wolf, "Steve Jobs: The Next Insanely Great Thing," *Wired*, February 1996. http://archive.wired.com.

27. Quoted in Isaacson, *Steve Jobs*, p. 43.

28. Quoted in Goodell, "The Steve Jobs Nobody Knew."

Chapter Two: Founding Apple Computer

29. Intel, "The Story of the Intel 4004." www.intel.com.

30. Blumenthal, *Steve Jobs: The Man Who Thought Different*, p. 55.

31. Quoted in John Markoff, "Steven P. Jobs, 1955–2011: Apple's Visionary Redefined Digital Age," *New York Times*, October 5, 2011. www.nytimes.com.

32. Steve Wozniak, with Gina Smith, *iWoz: Computer Geek to Cult Icon: How I Invented the Personal Computer, Co-Founded Apple, and Had Fun Doing It*. New York: W.W. Norton, 2006, pp. 150–51.

33. Quoted in Isaacson, *Steve Jobs*, p. 60.

34. Wozniak, with Smith, *iWoz*, p. 166.

35. Quoted in Isaacson, *Steve Jobs*, p. 61.

36. Wozniak, with Smith, *iWoz*, p. 172.

37. Quoted in Isaacson, *Steve Jobs*, p. 63.

38. Quoted in Blumenthal, *Steve Jobs: The Man Who Thought Different*, p. 61.

39. Quoted in Harry McCracken, "The Man Who Jump-Started Apple," *PC World*, August 23, 2007. http://web.archive.org.

40. Jobs, interview by Sheff, "Playboy Interview: Steve Jobs."

41. Quoted in Isaacson, *Steve Jobs*, p. 71.

42. Quoted in Christine Moorman, "Why Apple Is a Great Marketer," *Forbes*, July 10, 2012. www.forbes.com.

43. Quoted in Blumenthal, *Steve Jobs: The Man Who Thought Different*, p. 208.

44. Wozniak, with Smith, *iWoz,* p. 188.

45. Harry McCracken, "Apple II Forever: a 35th-Anniversary Tribute to Apple's First Iconic Product," *Time*, April 16, 2012. http://techland .time.com.

46. Jobs, interview by Morrow, "Excerpts from an Oral History Interview."

Chapter Three: Challenges

47. Wozniak, with Smith, *iWoz,* p. 225.

48. Quoted in Isaacson, *Steve Jobs*, p. 105.

49. Isaacson, *Steve Jobs,* p. 105.

50. Steve Lohr, "Creating Jobs," *New York Times*, January 12, 1997. www .nytimes.com.

51. Wozniak, with Smith, *iWoz,* p. 226.

52. Malcolm Gladwell, "The Tweaker," *New Yorker*, November 14, 2011. www.newyorker.com.

53. Quoted in Blumenthal, *Steve Jobs: The Man Who Thought Different*, p. 105.

54. Andy Hertzfeld, "The Father of the Macintosh," Folklore. www.folk lore.org.

55. Quoted in Isaacson, *Steve Jobs*, pp. 81–82.

56. Quoted in Isaacson, *Steve Jobs*, p. 84.

57. Quoted in Goodell, "The Steve Jobs Nobody Knew."

58. Quoted in Isaacson, *Steve Jobs*, p. 91.

59. Andy Hertzfeld, "The End of an Era," *Folklore*, May 1985. www.folklore.org.

60. Quoted in Blumenthal, *Steve Jobs: The Man Who Thought Different*, p. 128.

Chapter Four: Time Away from Apple

61. Quoted in Isaacson, *Steve Jobs*, p. 216.

62. Jobs, commencement address, Stanford University.

63. Quoted in Patricia Lakin, *Steve Jobs: Thinking Differently*. New York: Aladdin, 2011, p. 115.

64. Steve Jobs, interview by Gerald C. Lubenow, "Jobs Talks About His Rise and Fall," *Newsweek*, September 29, 1985. www.newsweek.com.

65. Jobs, interview by Lubenow, "Jobs Talks About His Rise and Fall."

66. Goodell, "The Steve Jobs Nobody Knew."

67. Tim Berners-Lee, "The WorldWideWeb Browser," World Wide Web Consortium. www.w3.org.

68. John Lasseter, interview by Stephanie Goodman, "Pixar's John Lasseter Answers Your Questions," *New York Times*, November 1, 2011. http://artsbeat.blogs.nytimes.com.

69. Jobs, commencement address, Stanford University.

70. Quoted in Lohr, "Creating Jobs."

71. Mona Simpson, "A Sister's Eulogy for Steve Jobs," *New York Times*, October 30, 2011. www.nytimes.com.

72. Simpson, "A Sister's Eulogy for Steve Jobs."

73. Quoted in Isaacson, p. 541.

74. Sheena Chestnut Greitens, "What Jobs Taught Me," *Newsweek*, October 10, 2011. www.newsweek.com.

Chapter Five: A Legacy of Innovation and Success

75. Quoted in John A. Byrne, *World Changers: 25 Entrepreneurs Who Changed Business as We Knew It.* New York: Penguin, 2011, p. 85.

76. John Sculley, interview by Leander Kahney, "John Sculley on Steve Jobs, the Full Interview Transcript," Cult of Mac, October 14, 2010. www.cultofmac.com.

77. Quoted in "Apple Presents iPod," press release, Apple, October 23, 2001. www.apple.com.

78. Lakin, *Steve Jobs: Thinking Differently*, p. 155.

79. Quoted in Ryan Block, "Live from Macworld 2007: Steve Jobs Keynote," *Engadget*, January 9, 2007. www.engadget.com.

80. Quoted in John D. Sutter and Doug Gross, "Apple Unveils the 'Magical' iPad," CNN, January 28, 2010. www.cnn.com.

81. Fred Vogelstein, "And Then Steve Said, 'Let There Be an iPhone,'" *New York Times*, December 4, 2013. www.nytimes.com.

82. Ifo Apple Store, "The Stores—a Concise Description." www.ifoapple store.com.

83. Isaacson, *Steve Jobs*, p. 455.

84. Jobs, commencement address, Stanford University.

85. Steve Jobs, "Letter from Steve Jobs," Apple Press Info, August 24, 2011. www.apple.com.

86. Quoted in Brad Stone and Adam Satariano, "Tim Cook Interview: The iPhone 6, the Apple Watch, and Remaking a Company's Culture," *Bloomberg Businessweek*, September 18, 2014. www.business week.com.

87. Simpson, "A Sister's Eulogy for Steve Jobs."

88. Apple, "Statement by Apple's Board of Directors," press release, October 5, 2011. www.apple.com.

89. Goodell, "The Steve Jobs Nobody Knew."

Important Events in the Life of Steve Jobs

1955
Steve Paul Jobs is born on February 24 in San Francisco and adopted by Paul and Clara Jobs.

1967
Jobs gets his first glimpse of a desktop computer at the Hewlett-Packard Explorer's Club.

1973
Jobs attends Reed College for one semester then drops out.

1976
Steve Jobs, Steve Wozniak, and Ron Wayne form Apple Computer.

1977
Apple Computer releases the Apple II, which sells extremely well.

1978
Lisa, Jobs's first daughter, is born.

1980
Apple becomes a public company.

1984
Apple releases the first Macintosh computer.

1985
Jobs announces that he is leaving Apple; He starts a new computer company called NeXT.

1986
Jobs buys the computer graphics division of Lucasfilm and names it Pixar Animation Studios.

1991
Jobs marries Laurene Powell in Yosemite National Park; his first son, Reed, is born.

1997
Jobs returns to Apple as interim CEO.

1998
Apple releases the iMac, which is the fastest-selling Mac in Apple's history.

2001
Apple releases the iPod music player.

2003
Apple opens the iTunes Music Store; Jobs is diagnosed with pancreatic cancer.

2007
Apple releases the iPhone.

2010
Apple releases the iPad.

2011
Jobs resigns as CEO of Apple; later that year he dies at age fifty-six due to complications caused by pancreatic cancer.

For Further Research

Books

Gearoge Beahm, ed., *I, Steve: Steve Jobs in His Own Words*. Chicago, IL: B2 Books, 2011.

Karen Blumenthal, *Steve Jobs: The Man Who Thought Different*. New York: Feiwel and Friends, 2012.

Walter Isaacson, *Steve Jobs*. New York: Simon & Schuster, 2011.

Patricia Lakin, *Steve Jobs: Thinking Differently*. New York: Aladdin, 2011.

Steve Wozniak, with Gina Smith, *iWoz: Computer Geek to Cult Icon: How I Invented the Personal Computer, Co-Founded Apple, and Had Fun Doing It*. New York: W.W. Norton, 2006.

Internet Sources

Malcolm Gladwell, "The Tweaker," *New Yorker*, November 14, 2011. www.newyorker.com/magazine/2011/11/14/the-tweaker.

Jeff Goodell, "The Steve Jobs Nobody Knew," *Rolling Stone*, October 27, 2011. www.rollingstone.com/culture/news/the-steve-jobs-nobody-knew-20111027.

Steve Jobs, interview by Gary Wolf, "Steve Jobs: The Next Insanely Great Thing," *Wired*, February 1996. http://archive.wired.com/wired/archive//4.02/jobs.html?person=steve_jobs&topic_set=wiredpeople.

Daniel Morrow, "Excerpts from an Oral History Interview with Steve Jobs," Smithsonian Institution, April 20, 2005. http://americanhistory.si.edu/comphist/sj1.html.

John Sculley, interview by Leander Kahney, "John Sculley on Steve Jobs, the Full Interview Transcript," Cult of Mac, October 14, 2010. www.cult ofmac.com/63295/john-sculley-on-steve-jobs-the-full-interview-tran script.

Mona Simpson, "A Sister's Eulogy for Steve Jobs," *New York Times*, October 30, 2011. www.nytimes.com/2011/10/30/opinion/mona-simpsons -eulogy-for-steve-jobs.html?pagewanted=all&_r=0.

Picture Credits

Andrea C. Nakaya, a native of New Zealand, holds a BA in English and an MA in communications from San Diego State University. She has written and edited more than thirty-five books on current issues. She currently lives in Encinitas, California, with her husband and their two children, Natalie and Shane.